D1107518

THROUGH LIONS GATE

Photographs by Ted Czolowski
Text by Anne Broadfoot

A pictorial tour of Greater Vancouver,

published by

THE VANCOUVER REAL ESTATE BOARD,

and

dedicated to its citizens

Sailing majestically through Lions Gate under the bridge of the same name, which arches over the First Narrows passage.

VANCOUVER

For centuries this land lay undisturbed but for the roar of turbulent mountain fed waters, the stir of wilderness creatures and the movements of its original Indian inhabitants.

Now it rings with the clatter of the city, the whistle of water craft, the rip of the logger's saw – a twenty-four hour hum of the activity of metropolitan life. Yet, one hundred and seventy five years ago this coast was not even charted and scarcely more than a century has passed since British Columbia was first settled.

In 1792 Captain George Vancouver, who had sailed with Captain Cook on his earlier voyages in search of the North West Passage, arrived once again in H.M.S. Discovery to chart this coastline for the Crown. Cook had sailed to Nootka on the West Coast of what is now Vancouver Island some years before and already a Fort had been established there, but of the mainland little was known. Captain Vancouver found no passage to the Atlantic but he did find, in his own words, ". . . the most lovely country."

In 1827 a major British Fort was constructed at Fort Langley, just thirty five miles from where Vancouver stands today, up that mighty trade artery, the Fraser River. The tradition of sea trade and travel still prevails, with steam and diesel where once there was oar, sail and paddle wheel.

At Fort Langley in 1858 Sir James Douglas, Governor of Vancouver Island, proclaimed the new colony of British Columbia. The Capital of this new colony was Queensborough, changed to New Westminster in 1859. The colonies of Vancouver Island and British Columbia were united in 1866, and in 1870 the Capital was moved to Victoria, which has remained the seat of provincial government ever since.

Down river from New Westminster a brawling, sprawling infant was born. It was officially laid out as "Granville Townsite" in 1870 but unofficially and affectionately known as "Gastown" after "Gassy Jack" Deighton, one of the first hotel keepers in the settlement.

When the Canadian Pacific Railway pushed across the mountains, Granville fought and won the battle to become Western terminus. The name of the city was then officially changed to Vancouver. The railway girdled a continent with its shining bands of steel and arrival of the first passenger train from Montreal in 1887 heralded a new era of growth and settlement for Vancouver. Gold discoveries on Vancouver Island and in the Kootenays started the influx and the Klondyke strike of 1897 launched Vancouver into world importance as the point of departure to the Northern gold fields.

In the early 1900's a carriage and pair was the stylish mode of travel on Vancouver streets. Sawmills operated on Main Street; the corner of Granville and Georgia was dense forest with trees eleven feet in diameter. It was a day's journey by horse and cart to visit friends in the 'farming areas' of West Point Grey and Mount Pleasant.

Today, Vancouver city covers an area of 44 square miles. Monumental buildings and pleasant homes have replaced acres of forest in less than one hundred years. Major corners are equipped with blinking red and green traffic controls and industrialization has catapulted us into the electronic age. This growing metropolis is a lasting monument to those pioneer men of vision who looked beyond the wilderness and saw a city.

Greater Vancouver lies in an extravagently beautiful setting on the Western coast of Canada. Eight hundred thousand residents enjoy a year-round temperate climate with most winter weather above freezing and summers ranging in the seventies.

A public viewpoint on the 19th floor of the B.C. Hydro Building affords this exciting view of the Vancouver Hilton Hotel against a backdrop of mountains. In the background the marble turreted Marine Building, built in the early thirties, contrasts sharply with the architecture of the sixties.

Sea and rail travel meet and complement each other on the shores of Vancouver Harbour. 21,400 vessels clear port facilities each year, making the Port of Vancouver the busiest on the Pacific Coast. Above, freighters lie alongside with the Second Narrows Bridge and Burnaby Mountain rising in the background.

Below, pleasure craft in Coal Harbour are dwarfed by the city rising above. Yachts are moored in the marina surrounding the luxurious Bayshore Inn, centre front.

The downtown peninsula is the heart of this thriving metropolitan body, with bridges acting as arteries, pumping the ebb and flow of traffic into Vancouver centre. The Burrard Bridge, on the left, funnels traffic from the University and Dunbar area into the city. The Granville Bridge, centre, handles the bulk of north-south traffic. Four other bridges serve this central island.

In honour of the 1958 Centennial, Vancouver's Maritime Museum was built on the waterfront at the foot of Cypress Street.

The modern museum shows exhibits relating to man and the sea. Preserved in dry dock is the famous R.C.M.P. vessel St. Roch, historic Canadian Arctic schooner that twice conquered the North West Passage. It is seen here in one of the last photos taken before being covered by an A-frame building in early 1966.

In adjacent Hadden Park stands a one hundred foot totem, a replica of the one presented to Queen Elizabeth to mark B.C.'s 1958 Centennial.

A reminder of man's constant fascination with the sea – a romance started in the days of sail and still alive today when atomic powered vessels laugh at the trade winds. Vancouver's Maritime Museum displays this age-old symbol of sailing ships and sailing men – a gigantic anchor from a 19th century ship lost on this, the coast of the new world.

A family takes advantage of the evening sun to enjoy supper at Spanish Banks, named in honor of the Spanish captains who once claimed sovereignty of these lands for Spain. Though England successfully challenged their claim, and rights were presented to Captain Vancouver peacefully, Spain left her mark. Juan de Fuca's Strait, and Spanish Banks are names to remind us that Spanish seafarers were among the first white men to explore this new world.

Today Spanish Banks is a recreational paradise. Clear tidal water sweeps in over a sandy sea bottom that slopes gently for hundreds of yards, offering safe, enjoyable swimming. Vancouver Park Board continually updates facilities, providing plenty of parking and reclaiming more sandy beaches for public use.

In the distance the rising towers of apartments and growing residential districts of West Vancouver nestle at the foot of the Coast Range mountains. The Squamish tribes named the mountain formation 'The Sleeping Beauty', imagining the highest rise on the left to be the head, and the other formations to the right the rest of the body of an Indian Princess preserved in everlasting sleep.

The blue vastness of the Coast Mountains goes on to infinity in this air view taken at 9,000 feet. North Vancouver city huddles at their feet. Grouse Mountain's famous chair lift snakes up the peak left centre front, and Lynn and Seymour Canyons beckon the wanderer ever onward.

A great city rises from the shores of Lost Lagoon, bottom, and English Bay, centre right, marching off into the distance as it continues to grow. False Creek on the right winds its way under the many bridges leading to the city centre.

A spot of quiet repose within sight and sound of the bustling city streets. A boy watches breakers rolling in from their mysterious Pacific beginnings.

Bathers on Kitsilano Beach look out at the blue Pacific, or turn to the impressive sight of this modern city growing into one of the most important centres in the Dominion.

At the right, an unusual sunset shot from Kitsilano Pool, showing the small-craft launching platform in stark relief against a golden sea and sky.

Evening walk along English Bay Beach.

Children journey back to the age of steam as they play on Engine 374, the first engine to make the pioneer mountain railway crossing to B.C. in 1887. It is now enshrined forever at Kitsilano Beach Park.

Since 1911 the bandstand at Alexandra Park has stood overlooking English Bay on a tiny island of grass now surrounded by high rise apartments. It is a memento of more leisurely days, offering a respite still to those who love the sound of a band concert on the cool of a summer's evening. Above, the bandstand plays host to the displays of Vancouver's professional art colony, holding an exhibition in the open air.

An arboretum at Queen Elizabeth Park, features many coastal trees and shrubs, lawns, flower gardens and landscaped streams.

Weeping willows and a rambling stream create a quiet glade where visitors find relaxation from everyday cares.

QUEEN ELIZABETH PARK

Little Mountain, off Cambie and Thirty Third Avenue, is on the highest point in Vancouver, 410 feet above sea level at the Observation Post. Queen Elizabeth Park was developed from old gravel diggings into one of the most beautiful spots in the city. It provides a panoramic view of homes, harbour and North Shore mountains.

Golfers enjoy year-round golfing in the West Coast's temperate climate. There are eight private Golf Courses and eight public links on the lower mainland, with two public pitch and putt courses for fun and practice and a number of practice driving ranges, as well as the Peace Portals Public Course in Peace Park, on the International Boundary between British Columbia and Washington State.

PACIFIC RAIDER

The north arm of the Fraser River is home port to many Coastal fishing vessels. Here, at the foot of Blenheim Street, as many as seventy-five trawlers, seiners, packers, whalers and supply boats can be seen at one time, tied up wintering or undergoing repairs.

UNIVERSITY OF BRITISH COLUMBIA

The University of British Columbia received its charter in 1908, enrolled its first class of students in 1915 in the Fairview District, and has been on the present site in West Point Grey since 1925.

From small beginnings, the University now has 16,000 students trooping to the 2,500 acre campus each September for basic arts and sciences, law, medicine, dentistry, engigineering, commerce and business administration, forestry, agriculture, education, home economics, physical education, social work, architecture and nursing. Undergraduate and post graduate programs are also carried out, as well as research and teaching in such typically British Columbian areas as mining, metallurgy, fisheries, oceanography and forestry. The Real Estate industry in British Columbia created an education "first" in 1958 when it established a Chair in Estate Management through the Faculty of Commerce and Business Administration at UBC.

Winter sessions are held from September til April. During July and August, UBC operates extensive summer sessions for academic credit courses, plus a non-credit summer school of the arts operated by the Extension Department. Students from all over the world travel to B.C. to study and International House records show a growing attendance of foreign students.

Private residences on the Endowment Lands are among the loveliest in the city. 18 hole golf course is also located on the Endowment Lands.

The University houses approximately 3,000 students in ultra modern residences. More dormitory facilities are added each year to handle the burgeoning out-of-town student body.

The original University buildings, mellowed with time, blend with the architecture of the sixties to produce one of the most beautiful campuses in Canada. When visiting here you should park your car and walk the malls and boulevards to discover for yourself the many sights the University has to offer.

TOTEM POLE PARK

The original idea of the Totem Pole Park started with the restoration and installation of various tribal totem poles and house poles in the University collection. Totem poles are unique to the northwest coast of British Columbia and southern Alaska. They are carved to represent some real or mythical event in a family history. The occasion of erecting a totem pole was one of elaborate celebration and an important social triumph.

Contrary to popular belief, totems were not idols and were not worshipped! Especially commissioned artists carved the poles in logs of red cedar, putting on them the symbolic animals and humans which represented incidents and ancestors in a family history. Although individual figures may be identified by each pole, it is not easily possible to recount the history depicted on a pole without knowing the peoples and events portrayed there.

At the southwest corner of the park there is a Kwakiutl section, completed in 1953. This section also contains carvings and structures representing the tribal traditions of the Haida of the Queen Charlotte Islands.

In 1959, William Reid undertook completion of the Haida collection. Mr. Reid was a well known craftsman in silver, and studied further under famous Indian carver, the late Chief Mungo Martin, in Victoria. Douglas Cranmer of Alert Bay, also a student of Mungo Martin, took part in the project which took two and one-half years to complete. The carvings and buildings represent a small segment of a Haida village.

NITOBE GARDEN

The Nitobe Memorial Garden was designed by Professor Kannosuke Mori of Chiba University, Japan, and is dedicated to the memory of Dr. Inazo Nitobe, a distinguished educator and international civil servant who died in Victoria in 1933. Dr. Nitobe had spent many years furthering Japanese Canadian relationships.

In recognition of his distinguished international service, the Japan Society of Vancouver gave a stone lantern to the University, which is now in a place of honor in the Memorial Garden.

This garden is a combination of a tea garden surrounding the tea-house, and a landscape garden called a "circulating garden" which should be viewed from any point of the circulating path and not only from one spot.

The tea garden is a rock garden featuring abstract design of rocks, carefully chosen to harmonize in proportion and shape. Moss softens the outlines, and stepping stones form decorative features.

The garden simulates nature in miniature, with an artificial 'mountain', waterfall, and lake.

Six types of lanterns are seen. The Yukimi, or snow view lantern on the island in the lake is so called because its beauties are thought to be greatest under a thin coat of snow.

A guide is on hand to explain features of the garden to weekend visitors.

VANCOUVER RELAXES

The choice is varied – go down to the sea in ships of any size; go up the slopes on skis (or just up the chairlift to dine 2,500 feet above the city); swim in the sea or many outdoor pools in season, or the indoor pools when the weather's cool; golf at one of eight public or eight private courses, or fish the many streams and lakes or the sea surrounding Vancouver. A multitude of activities await the outdoor enthusiast – most of them within an hour's drive (or less) from any given point.

There's entertainment too, from top flight travelling Broadway productions to opera, folk festivals, travel films and local professional theatre, all seen at the Queen Elizabeth Theatre in the heart of downtown Vancouver. Movies make big news with glossier, more glamorous surroundings than ever before. There are cocktail lounges and private clubs all over the city and coffee houses and ethnic clubs for specialty seekers.

Vancouver has grown up to the pleasures of dining. You'll find Italian foods, southern fried chicken, East Indian foods, Greek, Polynesian, steak houses and seafood restaurants.

This is one of the few remaining "night club circuit" cities in North America, with regular visits by the greats and soon-to-be-greats of the entertainment world at three city night clubs.

This is the home of the Lions Football Club and the Mounties baseball team. Racing fans mingle with pigskin fans at Exhibition Park where the ponies are still running when the football season begins. The Pacific National Exhibition each August is ten days of agricultural fair, trade fair and fun fair combined. All summer long the gayway delights young and old at Exhibition Park.

Looking for a special kind of atmosphere? Vancouver's Chinatown is second only in size to San Francisco's – with the finest cuisine available in Oriental splendor that boggles the imagination of the uninitiated.

When you're in the mood to go shopping, visit the oriental bazaars of Chinatown, or savor the continental flavor of European shops on Robson "strasse"; English and Irish imports dominate the scene in elegant mid-town shops and all around the City you'll find countless specialty shops, department stores and shopping plazas where the world's products and produce are displayed – all doing their part in creating the special atmosphere that is this magnificent seaport city, Vancouver, British Columbia.

Granville Street at night.

Chinatown glows with neon color as night falls.

PACIFIC NATIONAL EXHIBITION

The earliest exhibition in the city of Vancouver was held in 1910. It was developed mainly as an agricultural show, and this still remains a big part of the fourteen day Pacific National Exhibition as it is held today. In the sixties, Exhibition visitors enjoy the permanent gayway, as well as displays of home and agricultural arts, trade and industry, science and stage shows. In this aerial view of Exhibition Park you see the many permanent buildings and the existing sports facilities, including, 5¼ furlong race track featuring three months of pari-mutuel racing each year and 38,000-seat Empire Stadium, home of professional football.

A day at the Fair.

The coastal climate is ideal for gardening, producing a year-round lushness unequalled anywhere in Canada. The heritage of evergreen growth is seen in trees and shrubs around the city, glowing green on the dullest winter day. Bulbs start blooming in early spring, and every kind of flower, tree and shrub abound in public parks and private gardens throughout the year.

STANLEY PARK

Captain Vancouver and his men were the first Europeans to see the beautiful solitude of Vancouver harbour; the first to see Stanley Park in all its stately grandeur: a dense, silent forest, home of the gentle Squamish and habitat of wild animals.

On June 13th, 1792, they passed through First Narrows amid a shower of soft white waterfowl feathers – an honored welcome from the natives. They found no channel leading to the Atlantic, which was the purpose of their voyage, but they ushered in an era of change for a land that had lain silent for thousands of years.

Captain Vancouver thought the peninsula now called Stanley Park was an Island lying across First Narrows, with a second channel through Lost Lagoon, its entrance just behind a smaller island now known as "Deadman's", but in fact, the "channel" was the end of an arm of the very harbour where he was anchored.

Soon men of vision began arriving and settling the coast and foretold a great city rising like magic on the shoreline and beyond. In the 1850's, Engineer F. Brockton, of the Survey Ship HMS "Plumper", discovered coal on the south shore of Burrard Inlet – hence the name Coal Harbour. In 1863 the Royal Engineers charted the entire coastline of this important coal peninsula and marked off a large tract of 1,000 acres as "reserve" in the name of the Crown for military use to defend the capital city, New Westminster, from hostile attack from the rear.

In 1886 Vancouver was already a bustling centre and its citizens petitioned the Government for control of the reserve as a park. Permission was granted so on September 27th, 1888, His Worship Mayor Oppenheimer officially opened and named the park, calling it "Stanley" after Lord Stanley, then Governor General of Canada.

A statuette in bronze bears Lord Stanley's own dedication – "To the use and enjoyment of people of all colours, creeds and customs for all time." A bridge was built over Coal Harbour to allow people to attend the park's opening ceremonies held on the site of an Indian village near Prospect Point. This was the home of Chief Khat-sah-lanogh, who was later honored in the naming of a residential suburb – "Kitsilano."

The fountain at Lost Lagoon was built in 1936 for the park's Golden Jubilee celebrations. The name "Lost Lagoon" was coined by Indian poetess, E. Pauline Johnson, who lived in Vancouver's west end. On sunny afternoons she liked to paddle her canoe in Coal Harbour, the tip of which was still an arm of the sea. One day she arrived at an unusually low tide to find only acres of mud flat. She was so chagrined she penned the poem "It is dusk on the lost lagoon." The name stuck even after considerable park development, and construction of the causeway completely closed the 'arm' away from the sea. Today, the lagoon never disappears – it remains a source of beauty and pleasure to the city of Vancouver and its world renowned Stanley Park.

Burrard Yacht Club boathouses in Coal Harbour, overshadowed by the metropolitan Vancouver skyline.

The Stanley Park Causeway, entrance to 1,000 acres of the most beautiful park in B.C., and also route to Lions Gate Bridge and the North Shore.

Along the park drive to Brockton Point stand totems of the Squamish Indians, the "canoe Indians", a memorial to the first residents of this coast.

In 1888 the sound of the lassies of the Salvation Army singing "Hallelujah, Hallelujah" could be clearly heard across the still water from what was then called "Hallelujah Point". For the past 70 years Vancouverites have set their clocks by the 9 o'clock gun, which booms its time signal across the Harbour from the same park location.

From Brockton Point Light, look out to sea, and the wonders of the present, or reflect on the past, when pioneers of Granville, Moodyville and Hastings Townsite were interred in this area, one of Vancouver's first graveyards. No burials took place after 1886 and all evidence of its hallowed use has disappeared from this ground.

A figurehead from the old Empress of Japan, one of history's proudest passenger vessels which called regularly in Vancouver, is permanently established along the Park Drive.

The Children's Zoo, opened in its present spot in 1964, gives children a chance to pet and play with child-size animals.

The miniature railway leaves from "Stanley Park Junction" around a horseshoe shaped ¾-mile right-of-way through forest, through a miniature tunnel, over a bridge, along the shore of a lake stocked with wild fowl, and bordered by Indian teepees, a forest fire lookout, and gold mining waterwheel.

A prehistoric Indian village built of thick cedar slabs cut with stone hammers and chisels was once located on this site, a fitting place for Lumberman's Arch, memorial to the industry that helped make the Pacific Northwest grow and prosper.

Lumberman's Arch Pool is built on the site of an ancient Indian Midden where acres of shells were dug up in 1888 to surface the first park-girdling carriage-way known as the "Park Road".

Penguins lend their special dignity to a zoo outing. The monkey and sea lion enclosure draws young and old, while a quiet glade attracts a strolling couple. The Vancouver Public Aquarium, world acclaimed marine exhibit, seems to take second place here to the lure of a mounted Park Policeman.

Polar bears in the zoo tumble and play joyfully, entertaining crowds of delighted visitors.

Along the avenue of flowering Japanese cherry trees, a quiet stroll brings you to the Japanese memorial erected to honor Japanese-Canadians who died in the First World War.

A sensational display of blooms await the visitor in the Rose Gardens. From early in the spring, visitors and camera fans are bewitched by every type and color of bloom.

The Stanley Park Pavilion, where you enjoy full restaurant facilities, and a quiet respite in a verdant setting.

Beaver Lake, originally called "Ahka-Chu", 'a little lake', by the Squamish tribes, displays its beauty to visitors. Here lily pads float over the surface, giving food and shelter to many water fowl. Feeding the ducks is a favored pastime by residents and visitors.

Lions Gate Bridge, gateway to the North Shore, built in 1938 by the Guinness family to serve their British Properties land investments.

Stanley Park's first residents are honored with totems preserving their historical memory. Here, a tall totem at Prospect Point.

Further along the Park Drive, "the big tree", a tourist attraction since 1900. It was burned by some unknown fire but still stands to delight the camera fan.

LEFT: Third Beach, one of the many public beaches that line the park. CENTRE: Siwash Rock, the legendary "Slah-Kay-Ulsh", who was an Indian turned to stone on the beach as punishment for his greed and thoughtlessness. RIGHT: Sunlight beams through branches of the park trees she loved so well, on a memorial to famous poetess, E. Pauline Johnson, who died in Vancouver in 1913.

The sea wall which will eventually girdle the park, forms a pleasant pathway for strollers. In the building for roughly 40 years, this granite wall now stretches from HMCS Discovery around the park.

Ferguson Point Tea House, another long time fixture in the Stanley Park facilities. The Spanish navigator, Narvaez, 1791, called this point Punta de la Bodega. As he did not enter the First Narrows, he believed Stanley Park was joined to West Vancouver.

Second Beach, where the sand is mechanically sifted each season, provides excellent seaside bathing. It was called "Stait Wouk" by the Squamish, the place where they obtained a special clay they burned into white chalk which was used to clean fur blankets.

Lost Lagoon Park, the place for a stroll beside a rambling brook, a picnic on the grass or a rest in the shade, also offers a popular pitch and putt golf course.

Seek and find relaxation only a few blocks from the hustle and hurry of the city. Buildings rise beyond the trees, but here the pace is restful and quiet.

Apartment Houses rise above Lost Lagoon – a far cry from only 100 years ago when split cedar slab lodges housed the proud and independent Squamish band.

The arch of a bridge, the colors of nature, and her most graceful creatures too – a sight to see on Lost Lagoon creek any day of the week.

"What an object lesson of peace is shown today by our two countries to all the world. No grim-faced fortifications mark our frontiers; no huge battleships patrol our dividing waters; no stealthy spies lurk in our tranquil border hamlets. Only a scrap of paper, recording hardly more than a simple understanding, safeguards lives and properties on the Great Lakes, and only humble mile posts mark the inviolable boundary line for thousands of miles through farm and forest. Our protection is our fraternity, our armour is our faith, the tie that binds more firmly year by year is ever-increasing acquaintance and comradeship through interchange of citizens and the compact is not of perishable parchment, but of fair and honorable dealing, which, God grant, shall continue for all time."

This is the text of the memorial in Stanley Park, erected by Kiwanis International in memory of the visit of President Warren Harding, 29th President of the United States, on July 26th, 1923.

WEST VANCOUVER

A short drive from downtown Vancouver, across the Lions Gate Bridge, you enter a recreational wonderland – hiking trails, picnic areas, yachting and boating, fishing streams, scenic tours – all within minutes of a mid-town hotel or a cross-town home.

You arrive first at the growing community of West Vancouver which began on the day in 1905 when John Lawson ferried his family and possessions – even his cow – from Stanley Park in a rowboat. The settlers came then, and it grew from a summer community to the elite residential area you see today, served by excellent highways and flanked by the magnificence of nature – the blue Pacific and the misty peaks.

West Vancouver has an area of 34 square miles and is bounded on the North by the mountains of the Coast Range; on the East by the District of North Vancouver; on the South by the waters of Burrard Inlet and on the West by Howe Sound.

In West Vancouver you can shop in Western Canada's most modern shopping complex; stop at Ambleside Park for tennis and a children's playground; rest on the sandy beach or bathe in the sea. Visit Lighthouse Park, a beautiful wooded natural park. Fisherman's Cove shelters all manner of craft and good sport fishing abounds in the waters around the Cove. Gleneagles Golf & Country Club welcomes visiting golfers, and Whytecliff Park offers a magnificent view of the sea. Horseshoe Bay has an excellent picnic area, shady trees and bathing beach, and power and row boats for fishing are available for rent. The mountain walls that shelter the Bay give on to the open waters of Howe Sound – route of those lumbering ladies of transport – government auto and passenger ferries which travel to Vancouver Island and other coastal points.

P. & O. Orient Lines luxury vessel clears the Lions Gate Bridge, outward bound from Vancouver Harbour on its journey to other famous world ports.

As you cross Lions Gate Bridge you have a gull's eye view of sweeping beaches, some of the city's finest homes, and range upon range of mountains marching away in the distance. This view is the harbinger of spectacular views to come as you follow Marine Drive along its winding coastline route.

From Marine Drive you see beautiful homes perched dramatically on the very edge of the sea.

A wooded glade in the heart of a busy area – a remote spot in West Vancouver's lovely Lighthouse Park.

Lighthouse Park juts into the sea between Caulfield Cove and Howe Sound. Inviting footpaths welcome the adventurous wanderer and you get a closeup view of Point Atkinson Light House, which has served as a Coastal sentinel and warning to B.C. shipping for over half a century.

Eagle Harbour, facing the Straits of Georgia, offers berthing for a variety of small boats and wide sandy beaches make it a pleasant spot for a day's recreation.

Fisherman's Cove, where it is said the salt sea air brings out the sailor in the most hidebound landlubber. Guardian mountains keep this cove a peaceful, protected retreat for pleasure boat owners.

Gleneagles – 46 acres of well tended golf course, is surrounded by sea and mountains. This course will challenge the most experienced golfer but its beauty will make up for even the highest score.

Whytecliff Park – hiking trails, boat rental, bathing beach and children's playground, and this inviting lookout where you can view the grandeur of Howe Sound.

A B.C. Government Ferry arrives at Horseshoe Bay from Vancouver Island. Horseshoe Bay affords a fine opportunity for boating and fishing.

Take a breathtaking drive along scenic route #99, a splendid paved highway carved out of mountain sides and bordered by Howe Sound. The Upper Levels Seaview Drive takes you 28 miles to Britannia Beach and Squamish, leads you to the lovely Alice Lake trailer camp, and is climaxed when you arrive at the Paradise Valley resort, where nature's ultimate beauty and Western hospitality are combined.

From high up on Eagle Ridge the boats at Fishermen's Cove look like toys at anchor.

You look down upon bustling coastal traffic as you follow the modern highway snaking down the cliffside to join the shore.

The Seaview Highway hugs the cliffs as it winds along its way to Squamish.

Browning Lake at Murrin Park, a popular picnic area, easily accessible to highway traffic.

Rising high above its sister peaks, Mt. Garibaldi overlooks the Seaview Highway.

Shannon Falls, cascading over 800 feet, before flowing into the waters of Howe Sound.

Squamish – centre of a logging and milling industry, viewed from the harbour and framed by mountains and mill-booms.

Coast range peaks look down on the swiftly running Squamish River, a popular fishing spot for residents and tourists.

Another spectacular mountain view seen from the highway to Alice Lake, pictured on the right

Paradise Valley – 46 scenic miles from Vancouver, where the Cheakamus River offers fishing for Dolly Varden and Steelhead.

A modern lodge provides excellent accommodation in this mountain-locked retreat.

Garibaldi Provincial Park, with its rugged mountain wilderness, opens unlimited opportunity for climbing, hiking, and skiing. In summer, fishing and swimming are also enjoyed.

Full tourist accommodation is available at Diamond Head, with its unique alpine setting and excellent ski area.

BRITISH PROPERTIES

A far sighted company, called the British Pacific Properties Ltd., backed by Guinness money, envisioned an executive housing development on the West Vancouver slopes and purchased and developed some 4000 acres of land, known as the "British Properties." To provide rapid access it built the Lions Gate Bridge, finished in 1937, and the first lots were put on sale in the Properties that year. Today it is one of the show places of Canada with a high concentration of the country's most opulent homes.

Approaching the Properties up Taylor Way you are greeted by a divided avenue of Japanese Flowering Cherry Trees, seen here in their colorful spring dress.

Mountainside living has produced some of the most unique architecture in Canada.
A few of the luxurious British Properties homes are pictured here.

Called one of the five most beautiful courses in North America, Capilano Golf and Country Club nestles in a scenic spot among evergreens and North Shore Mountains.

NORTH VANCOUVER

North Vancouver was born in 1891 spawned by a magnificent growth of timber and nurtured by the district's first industry – the Moodyville sawmills.

It was in these mills that the first electric lights north of San Francisco blinked on in 1882, a triumph of approaching civilization and industrialization.

At the turn of the century the North Shore was a popular summering spot but soon holidayers succumbed to the beauties of the area and stayed all year round. In 1907 the City of North Vancouver was incorporated.

Growth of the North Shore was hastened by the building of the first shipyards on the coast in North Vancouver. As Vancouver city grew, many people saw the advantages of living in this area with its spectacular view of harbour and mountains.

A view of wigwam and Indian carvings at Capilano Canyon Park. Below – Indian carvers from the nearby Capilano Reserve at work. To the right – a view of the swinging bridge known as the "8th Wonder of the World."

The world famous Capilano Suspension Bridge, 230 feet above the river, stretches 450 feet across the Capilano canyon, and has thrilled visitors since 1889.

Anglers on the edge of the Capilano River, fishing one of the many pools that harbor trout and steelhead.

The Cleveland Dam, completed in 1954, provides most of the water for greater Vancouver consumption. It was named after Ernest Albert Cleveland, the first Chief Commissioner of the Greater Vancouver Water District, who died in 1952.

The Lions – famed twin peaks overlooking Vancouver Harbour, seen from Cleveland Dam, with the Capilano Lake at their feet, clear mountain water held in reserve for the city's use.

The new gondola chairlift and the Grouse Mountain twin-seat chairlift – just 20 minutes from city centre – whisk you to the chalet atop the mountain. From the summit you see the magnificent panorama of the city, ringed by the harbour, the delta of the Fraser River, the green Fraser Valley farmlands, and bordered by the peaks of the Vancouver Island Mountains to the west, the Coast Range to the east, and the Olympics to the south. Ski facilities are also to be found on neighbouring Seymour and Hollyburn Mountains.

LYNN VALLEY

Lynn Valley, in North Vancouver, is another growing residential area and boasts one of the Lower Mainland's most beautiful natural parks – Lynn Canyon Park.

A swinging suspension bridge crosses Lynn Creek which gushes through a deep gorge cut through rugged rock. Hiking trails wind through nature's unspoiled wonderland, picnic areas and tearoom enhance the park area for many visitors.

Deep chasms and gushing waterfalls seen from the swinging bridge give you a feeling of nature's never-changing beauty. Quiet pools provide an opportunity for swimming or fishing.

DEEP COVE

From Deep Cove Marina, a view up the Indian Arm – tranquil waters and eye-filling vistas of towering mountains. Deep Cove itself is a delightful summer resort located in a protected bay on the North Arm of Burrard Inlet at the eastern end of North Vancouver. Swim from smooth beaches, picnic, fish, hike, or take to the water in rental boats from this busy tourist centre.

BURNABY

When the Crown Colony of British Columbia was established in 1858, Burnaby as we know it today was a vast area of unincorporated Crown Land. Queensborough was soon established where the Brunette River emptied into the Fraser. This same Brunette River meandered through the Crown Lands to its source in a lake called Burnaby. Indians camped along the Brunette's banks while the few white settlers hugged the Fraser's shores or stayed in Queensborough, soon renamed New Westminster.

The first road built for the use of settlers in New Westminster started at the Brunette River and extended north to Burrard Inlet. This road is now called North Road and has become the eastern boundary of Burnaby. A small settlement of whites soon stretched out on either side of this road.

In 1859 an access was finished to Burnaby Lake and more people moved in to open up this area. Construction of the Central Park tramline in 1894 induced the government of B.C. to subdivide land lying between the present Patterson and Royal Oak Avenues. Because heavily bushed, some of this land sold for only $60.00 an acre, and a number of settlers soon became established.

In June, 1892, a public meeting was called to consider plans for forming a new municipality. A resolution was adopted to "form a Municipality named Burnaby, embracing all the portion of the District of New Westminster lying between the boundaries of the cities of New Westminster and Vancouver, and the Fraser River and any other adjacent parts of the district not included in existing municipalities surrounding lands desired to be included in the new corporation."

The district received its charter in September, 1892, with an assessed value of $1,249,982 and a population of approximately 250. In 1966, total assessed value of municipal lands stands at $352,990,603 with an estimated population in excess of 110,000.

Today, Burnaby Lake in spring, before its mantle of water lilies have burst into bloom. Boat racing tracks are kept cleared of lilies. The Port Mann Freeway provides a speedy link between Vancouver and Fraser Valley points.

A monument to the faith of its citizens after 100 years in the Crown Colony of British Columbia, Centennial Pavilion, Burnaby's tribute to the Provincial Centennial celebrations in 1958.

An aerial view over Deer Lake looking past the Port Mann Freeway to the slopes of North Burnaby with Burrard Inlet showing faintly in the distance.

More indication of the growth, potential, and farsightedness of Corporation of Burnaby – Simon Fraser University, opened for inaugural classes in 1965, rises above the tree tops on Burnaby Mountain.

New Westminster City Hall.

NEW WESTMINSTER

Hudson's Bay traders had built Fort Langley, and sent out the first shipment of smoked and salted salmon from the area by 1830. As years passed and evidence of the value of this new land increased, Queen Victoria ordered Col. Richard Clement Moody and a company of Royal Engineers to Fort Langley as protection for the settlers and for survey and settlement purposes.

When British Columbia was officially declared a British Colony in 1858, governmental administration was centred at the Fort. But in 1859, under Col. Moody, the Royal Engineers began clearing the site for the new Colonial Capital on what is now Sapperton, along the shore of the Fraser River. Governor James Douglas asked Queen Victoria to name the new Capital, in the interim called "Queensborough" and in July of 1859, the Governor issued a proclamation that ". . . the Queen has been graciously pleased to decide the Capital of British Columbia shall henceforth be called "New Westminster."

On July 16th, 1860, New Westminster was incorporated as a city and the first Legislative Council of British Columbia was elected. It met in 1864 in the former barracks of the Royal Engineers. The seat of government was moved to Victoria in 1868, but by this time industrial development was on its way and New Westminster did not suffer from losing its prominence as Colonial Capital.

In 1867 the first successful experiments in hermetical sealing of salmon were carried out and the first cannery established in 1870. The Fraser Valley, then as now, had developed into one of the richest most fertile valleys in the world, with mixed farming, dairying, fruits and poultry, playing an important part in the economic growth of New Westminster, industrial centre of the Valley. Sawmills were established in the early 1870's and some 4,500 persons are now employed in this industry alone. The Fraser was the main sockeye salmon river and though fishermen now have turned to other Northern Rivers and deepsea fishing, the Fraser still leads the industry. 3,000 fishermen live in suburbs along the Lower Fraser where they moor their gillnetters, seiners and trollers.

The Port of New Westminster, a freshwater ice-free deepsea port, is 23 miles from the Gulf of Georgia up the South Arm of the Fraser River. Sternwheel river boats carried the earliest products down river in the 1800's, but today an average of 400 deepsea vessels enter the port annually from all countries of the world.

New Westminster, overlooking the Patullo Bridge link on Highway 99A to the U.S. Border crossing at Blaine, 18 miles away. In the distance is the Port Mann Bridge. In the foreground is the Royal Towers Hotel with Canada's only outdoor glass elevator.

The Garden of Friendship, presented to the City of New Westminster by its Sister City, Moriguchi, Osaka, Japan. The formal Japanese garden was officially opened in September, 1963, by Moriguchi's Mayor. Rocks, bridges and special planting arrangements are designed to present an ever-changing aspect as you walk around the garden.

The Port of New Westminster, with deepsea freighters
loading. The Patullo Bridge spans the Fraser River in the background
arching high over a lower level railroad bridge.

RICHMOND

Richmond Municipality takes its name from the name of the farm of the first settler, a Cariboo gold miner named Hugh McRoberts, who carved a farm and home on the islands in the Fraser River Delta in 1862.

The islands were first known simply as McRoberts Islands, and then the smaller island was called Sea Island because at the time of year when tides were highest, the Island was virtually covered by 4 feet of water. When Colonel Moody was charting the Lower Mainland areas in the early 1860's, he called the largest Island "Lulu", in honor of Lulu Sweet, a popular actress of the day.

Hugh McRoberts planned the first dykes to keep the water from his farm, and so set the stage for development of the Delta Islands – still dyked against high tides. Hugh McRoberts' daughter Jennie named their farm "Richmond" after her home in Richmond, Parramatta, New South Wales, and so it was retained when the Municipality of Richmond was formed in 1879.

The first bridge to the islands was built in 1889 linking the fast developing farmlands to the mainland. Today, much of the farmland has been replaced by homes for the 49,500 residents of Richmond Municipality, and the original wooden bridge has been replaced by the magnificent Oak Street span, arching over the North Arm of the Fraser River, a part of the rapid-transit freeway that speeds traffic across the Island to the Deas Island tunnel under the South Arm of the Fraser, towards the Southern boundary between British Columbia and Washington State.

Fast developing Richmond still has its quiet, pastoral spots. Above, a farm beside a placid canal. Below, an open air market with produce fresh from the fields, a constant lure to the city dweller.

The mighty Fraser seems subdued as it winds serenely along its final passage to the Gulf of Georgia. The North and South Arms of the Fraser embrace Lulu and Sea Islands, providing a water highway to the farming, industrial and residential areas along its banks.

A jet airliner sinks down from an almost cloudless sky to Vancouver International Airport, located on Sea Island.

A monument to this age of jet fast air travel which has developed within the short span of one generation.

Steveston – anchorage for many fishing fleets that ply coastal waters.

DELTA

The Municipality of Delta was incorporated as a rural municipality on November 10th, 1879 by sixty residents of the area. Today, the municipality has a population of over 18,000 and is growing steadily.

Forty two thousand acres comprise the sunny Delta lands, known as the "doorstep" to Vancouver. Ladner is the Municipal seat and also a port on the Fraser River with a history that goes back to the 1870's. Ladner is a residential, commercial and light industrial community serving miles of fertile farmlands and a familiar port of call for many lower mainland sportsmen who hunt and fish on the Delta.

Many residential subdivisions are rising in the Municipality as people become aware of rapid transportation and the sunny climate. In the central region of the Delta, lowland peat bogs produce peat famous locally and in the United States.

Right: The Deas Island Tunnel, completed in 1959, runs a half mile under the south arm of the Fraser River. The Deas Thruway and Tunnel provide a fast transportation route to the U.S., Vancouver and the Vancouver International Airport.

Below: A typical Delta dairy herd and an aerial view of rich farm lands bordering on the Fraser.

Delta farmlands form a gentle patchwork of color – a pastoral section only a few minutes from the bustle of the city.

Only a short drive from the city on Highway 499 is the Tsawwassen Ferry Terminal, where B.C. Government ferries provide fast, efficient service to Vancouver Island and the Gulf Islands.

FRASER VALLEY

The Fraser River wends its way through gently rolling farmland in the Fraser Valley and a common sight is shown above, commercial fishing vessels tied up for a rest or repairs.

The river is roughly paralleled by the Lougheed Highway, which speeds you through the city and out into the lovely valley to Haney, Mission and beyond. At Haney, you'll find a turn onto another good road that takes you to Garibaldi Provincial Park.

Alouette Lake, calm and serene, attracts swimmers, boaters, picnickers and fishermen from miles around. Plenty of room here for family fun, with the surrounding vista of Garibaldi Park Mountains.

The entrance to Garibaldi Park – a provincial welcome.

FORT LANGLEY

35 miles from Vancouver, via a gleaming black-top highway – replacing the original wagon track, stands Fort Langley, the most historic outpost on the Lower Mainland, and now preserved as a National Historic Park.

At Fort Langley, founded in 1827, the traders and artisans of the Hudson's Bay Company established the first permanent British settlement on the Lower Mainland and it developed not only as an active fur trading post, but as the centre of a productive agricultural area as well.

It was from Fort Langley that the proclamation came making British Columbia a Crown Colony. And it was the Fort that afforded the scattered white settlers what protection and social life existed in those pioneer days.

The Fort presented an imposing appearance to Coastal Indians. The palisade was of heavy, split cedar logs pinned close together with stout wooden pegs. The logs were set into the ground so that the height of the palisade was roughly 18 feet. Three bastions, each armed with two 9-pounder cannon, guarded the corners of the Fort. Within the palisade, 15 buildings were arranged in the 660 ft. by 242 ft. area. These were Officers' Quarters, residences of the supervisor and Indian trader, the cooper, the boatbuilder, the blacksmith, dairyman, three labourers and stewards, the depot storehouse, shops of the Indian trader, carpenter, cookhouses, warehouses and storerooms.

During Provincial Centennial observances in 1958, Fort Langley was restored as a National Monument. Materials and construction techniques used in the restoration followed closely those used in the original construction. Logs of Western red cedar were squared with the broadaxe for sills, posts, plates, beams, wall-fittings and roof members and then dressed with an adze to fit together closely and provide smooth surfaces.

Complete restoration was impossible – a railroad now occupies some of the original area of the Fort. But as much of the palisade as possible was erected, one bastion and one two-story building were rebuilt. A second building – an original fort structure – was restored.

Views of the two-story "Big House" are shown. When you visit the Fort you travel quickly back into the romantic past when the trader, the voyageur and the settler opened this magnificent land.

The Peace Arch, on the boundary between Canada and the United States of America, is a testimonial to international friendship. A beautiful park spans the 49th parallel. It is maintained jointly by British Columbia and Washington State. The view, right, is taken from the American side with its memorable tribute saying in so few words what so many forget.

CHILDREN · OF · A · COMMON · MOTHER

INDEX

CREDITS

Lithographed in Vancouver Canada by Agency Press Limited □ Color Separations – Graphic Industries /